BORTHWICK INSTITUTE OF HIS
UNIVERSITY OF YORK

The Eighteenth-Century Church in Yorkshire. Archbishop Drummond's primary visitation of 1764

by

Judith Jago and **Edward Royle**
Centre for Eighteenth-Century Studies, University of York

BORTHWICK PAPER No. 95

First Published 1999
© David Jago and Edward Royle

ISSN: 0524–0913

The cover illustration is from the portrait of Archbishop Drummond at Bishopthorpe Palace and appears courtesy of his Grace the Archbishop of York.

The emblem on the front is a copy of the central boss in the roof of St Anthony's Hall and represents the pig, traditionally associated with St Anthony the Hermit.

Acknowledgements

I should like to thank the staff at the Borthwick Institute for their unfailing helpfulness and support during the course of this research and the Associated University Presses for giving me a free hand to draw on Judith Jago's work for this paper even though she had already submitted her thesis to them for publication. Finally I wish to thank David Jago for his enthusiastic support and encouragement.

Abbreviations

BIHR   Borthwick Institute of Historical Research

Preface

Judith Jago completed her D.Phil. on 'The Governance of the Georgian Church: Robert Hay Drummond of York and his Primary Visitation of 1764' at the University of York in 1994. Within a year she had died of cancer and, although her thesis was published as *Aspects of the Georgian Church* (Associated University Presses, 1997), her hopes of revising parts of her research for a Borthwick Paper were never realised. The present work is intended to fulfil that ambition. It draws on the many conversations we had during the years I supervised her research and on the databases she assembled containing details of the clergy replies to Drummond's articles of enquiry which were included in the thesis but not its published version. I have reworked her data and reinterpreted it in the light of my own research on religion in eighteenth-century Yorkshire. The result is a genuinely collaborative effort which I hope does justice to her posthumous contribution. Where I have drawn on sections of her research for background, I have provided page references to the published version of her thesis which will in turn lead the reader to the primary sources from which she took her information.

Edward Royle
York, 1999

The Eighteenth-Century Church in Yorkshire. Archbishop Drummond's primary visitation of 1764

Introduction

Robert Hay Drummond, who became archbishop of York in October 1761, conducted his primary visitation of the diocese in May and June 1764. Visitations were required by Canon Law every three years and were intended as an audit of the spiritual and material condition of the church in the diocese, with an enquiry into the conduct of parochial affairs. In preparation for the visitation, separate questionnaires were prepared in which the bishop or archbishop asked specific questions of parochial clergy and churchwardens. The replies of the clergy have survived for only two visitations of the York diocese in the mid-eighteenth century - Archbishop Herring's returns of 1743 and Archbishop Drummond's of 1764 - and no further clergy returns are extant until Archbishop Thomson's primary visitation in 1865. Since Herring's returns were published and commented upon by Ollard and Walker in 1929-31, historians' understanding of the eighteenth-century church has greatly changed.[1] The widely accepted view then was the one propagated by reformers in the Victorian period, who measured the previous century by their own standards and found it wanting. In 1934 Norman Sykes began a revisionist trend which has been reinforced by more recent scholarship, though not without some dissenting voices.[2]

A case study of the Yorkshire parishes of the diocese of York in the archdeaconries of York, Holderness and Cleveland provides a useful contribution to this evolving historiography, since the 617 parishes and chapelries from which clergy submitted the returns analysed in this study were sufficiently varied to make the three archdeaconries typical of much that was England as a whole.[3] The parishes ranged from large upland areas like Halifax, divided into many townships and chapelries, to small urban fragments of a few acres such as those clustered within the city walls of York. Scenes of early industrialisation with expanding populations, remote moorland parishes with shrinking numbers, rich agricultural parishes, urban centres of some of the largest towns in England, remote fishing villages - all made up the varied experience that was Yorkshire in the eighteenth century. The clergy who served these parishes were as varied as their surroundings: conscientious residents, non-resident pluralists, overstretched and penurious curates, upholders of the High Church tradition, enthusiastic Evangelicals, scholars and gentlemen, industrious and idle. The examples provided by a study of these returns are sufficiently varied to give a good impression of the nature of the Georgian church as a whole. Furthermore, when Drummond's returns are taken with those of Herring from two decades earlier, it is possible also to suggest whether any clear trends were developing in the mid-eighteenth century, whether the condition of the church as a whole was deteriorating as Ollard and Walker believed, or whether a more optimistic view should be taken.

Visitation returns provide a rich source, but they have their limitations. Though they were private communications from the clergy to their diocesan, they were transactions between unequals. The archbishop wished to know whether all was well, the clergy wished to assure him that all was well, and therein lies a problem. Reputations and careers might depend on giving a good impression to the archbishop at the visitation. Nevertheless, the range of answers in itself provides something of a solution. There are different ways of answering questions: the verbose and the evasive, the perfunctory and the elaborate, the detailed, the vague and the suspiciously too-detailed, the formulistic and the individualistic. A combination of statistical analysis and impressionistic evaluation can build a realistically plausible picture of the Georgian church.

The Visitation

Archbishop Drummond was one of those aristocrats who eased themselves back into the higher reaches of the Georgian church after the uncertainties of the Stuart period.[4] Born in 1711, the second son of the seventh Earl of Kinoull, he had inherited the Strathallan estates in Perthshire at the age of twenty-eight. The Duke of Newcastle, controller of ecclesiastical patronage and much else in the reign of George II, was his kinsman. Like many of his class he was educated at Westminster school and Christchurch, Oxford, to which, after the grand tour in the company of his cousin, the Duke of Leeds, he returned in 1735 to study divinity. He took his doctorate in 1745. Meanwhile he had been ordained deacon and priest on successive days in 1736, being then presented to the living of Bothall in Northumberland which he retained as a non-resident until his translation to York in 1761. The most formative event of his early career was as royal chaplain to George II during the Dettingen campaign of 1743, a physical experience which may have equipped him for the arduous tasks of later confirmation and visitation tours. He was to undertake these with greater enthusiasm than some of his more elderly and unfit episcopal colleagues. For, although Drummond was an aristocratic pluralist who owed his promotion to family connections, and who performed his expected political duties in the House of Lords as might be expected of a creature of the Duke of Newcastle, he was also a conscientious churchman and an effective administrator.

Drummond was also a Yorkshire landowner, with an estate at Brodsworth near Doncaster. This gave him a working knowledge of the county, enhanced by his undertaking a confirmation tour for the ailing Archbishop Gilbert in 1758. As aristocratic landowner and archbishop, he occupied a dual position in the county's social hierarchy. In administering his diocese as much from Brodsworth as from Bishopthorpe, he was hardly an absentee. Having risen to the bench of bishops with aristocratic ease in his late thirties, Drummond still had the advantage of youth when thirteen years later and within the space of a few months, Newcastle secured for him first Salisbury and then York. Still in the prime of his life, he at once set to work. On the one hand he determined to make Bishopthorpe Palace fit for a gentleman by adding a new gatehouse, stable block and west front, constructed in the latest gothick style. Bishopthorpe was made suitable for entertaining Lord Rockingham and other neighbouring aristocrats when visiting York race course, conveniently just down the road. On the other hand, the surviving paper work shows him getting to grips with the details of administering his diocese and preparing for his primary visitation.

He had already conducted three visitations, in 1749, 1753 and 1758, as Bishop of St Asaph, and he had available to him copies of the papers sent out to churchwardens by his predecessor, as well as Herring's primary visitation papers of 1743.[5] Indeed, the questions closely follow Herring's model though, unlike Herring, he wanted to know about Queen Anne's Bounty of which he was an unusually careful governor. The first two questions in the articles of enquiry concerned the population of the parish and the number of dissenting families; and the number of dissenters' meeting houses, frequency of meetings, size of congregations and names of teachers. The questioning then switched to schools and school teachers. Fourthly, the administration of endowments in general and of Queen Anne's Bounty in particular was enquired into. Attention then focused on pastoral care: was the incumbent resident and if not why not; was there a curate, where did he live and what was he paid? This naturally led on to the question of pluralism and the frequency of services. Implicit in these questions was a recognition by the man who had been a pluralist as Bishop of St Asaph that well-regulated pluralism was an acceptable fact of life. Drummond's stipend from St Asaph was about £1,400 a year, but he had seen no harm in taking an additional £280 a year from his cure at Bothall whilst providing a resident curate to whom he paid £34. 10.0.[6] Then came questions about the parishioners: baptisms, frequency and methods of catechising, frequency of and attendance at the Lord's Supper. Next the archbishop enquired about chapels of ease and how they were served; and, finally, the twelfth question was about the performance of public penances. If answered conscientiously and honestly, the questions elicited for the archbishop - and for the historian after him - a great deal of information about the operations of the Georgian church at the parochial level.

The visitation began at Doncaster on 7 May 1764. Following a sermon delivered by invitation by the vicar, those rectors and vicars summoned to Doncaster were required to present themselves to their diocesan in person, bringing with them - if not returned earlier - their completed replies to the articles of enquiry, their licences and testimonials to confirm their credentials, and their parish terriers describing their parsonages, church furnishings and other ecclesiastical property. Some clergy were excused attendance for what was held to be good reason. A few failed to attend without good reason and had to be reprimanded by letter afterwards. From Doncaster, the visitation proceeded by way of Rotherham, Wakefield, Leeds, Skipton and Ripon to York, which was reached on 18 May. Then, after a month's break, Drummond resumed his peregrination on 20 June at Beverley and, progressing by way of Hull, Scarborough, Malton and Thirsk, reached the end at Stokesley on 29 June before heading north to his Peculiar at Hexham for confirmations on 4 July.[7]

Church services

The most visible work of the parochial clergy was the provision of public worship on Sundays, and the expectation of the articles of enquiry was for two services, with one sermon in the morning. The two services were as set out in the Prayer Book. Morning service could be said at any time before about half-past one in the afternoon, depending on the weather, and how far the clergyman (and people) had to travel or what other duty he had to undertake before arriving in his parish. Evening service could be said any time after about half-past one and was invariably over before dark. Evening services in the sense of being held after dinner – which was eaten at about four o'clock in the afternoon – would have been very unusual. The form of the services also kept to the Prayer Book rubric. Elaborate singing and church organs were for cathedrals, not parish churches, where the chanting of the appointed psalm was the closest the congregation came to music. This was not always the wish of the congregation. John Mulso, rector of the large industrialising parish of Thornhill near Wakefield, was clearly having problems with the musical ambitions of his parishioners when he wrote to his archbishop in May 1764

> The younger part of my parishioners were very sollicitous [sic] for a Gallery, to assemble there together in, as a musical Band, to sing Psalms. Finding they had got the Consent of most of the Parishioners, I at last gave them mine; but upon Condition that they would confine themselves to plain parochial Psalmody. But they are growing impatient of this Restraint, & are every now & then introducing Anthems; and I suffer in their good Opinion by restraining them. They plead the Custom of some of the neighbourhood, and I assert that it is not Parochial Service. They promise Obedience, but with Reluctance.[8]

Drummond's note of his reply runs: 'I sent an answer by Mr Greenwood, C[urate], that I was totally against anything but the common Psalm singing.'

Analysis of the 617 returns shows the double Sunday service to have been the most common pattern of provision across Yorkshire with 265 (43 per cent) of parishes making this return. Moreover, all but forty of these had also been offering two services in 1743, indicating a solid core of parishes in the diocese with the required level of provision week by week and year by year. As might be expected, many of these double-service churches were in the largest and most populous parishes such as Almondbury, Birstall, Bradford, Dewsbury, Ecclesfield, Halifax, Huddersfield, Hull, Kirkburton, Leeds, Pontefract, Rotherham, Sheffield, Wakefield and Whitby – all of which had more than a thousand families. But also in many rural parishes, even some with fewer than fifty families, two services were the norm. One such was Middlesbrough which had only twelve families in 1764. In a further 257 churches (42 per cent) there was one service on a Sunday, 169 of which had also had one service in 1743. A further seventy-four (12 per cent) had only fortnightly services. In only nine were services as infrequent as once a month with a further four even less frequent than that. Eight clergy were ambiguous in their replies, or made no return or, in the case of Bessingby, held no services at all because the church had fallen down and the parishioners attended the weekly services held by the curate at Carnaby, a mile away.

One of the principal characteristics of parishes and chapelries with infrequent services was the smallness of their populations. The most populous area to be served by a church with services at only monthly intervals was St Leonard's, New Malton (about 200 families), one of two ancient chapels-of-ease in the parish of St Mary's, Old Malton (119 families and weekly services). Brotton chapel (92 families) similarly was a chapel-of-ease, this time in Skelton parish, while St Maurice, York (75 families), was one of two churches serving the parish of Holy Trinity, Goodramgate, with St Maurice, united in the amalgamation of York parishes in 1586. More typical were Thornton-le-Street (27 families), Throapham (22 families) and Drypool (30 families), all served by clergy resident in slightly larger neighbouring parishes. Those churches in which a Sunday service was said at fortnightly intervals were more varied in their nature, though again smallness of population appears to have been their most common factor. Of the seventy-four parishes and chapelries in question, only ten churches served populations of more than a hundred families. The largest populations were those associated with the chapelry of St Michael, New Malton, and the parish church at Osmotherley (each with 230 families). Of the remaining churches, over two-thirds (43) served and probably met the needs of less than fifty families each.

The City of York was a special case, with 2,701 families in twenty-two parishes, thirteen of them wholly within the city walls and the rest with their populations largely within the walls. No church offered more than one service, as the incumbent at St Crux explained, 'divine service being performed at halfe the churches in York in the morning, and by the other halfe in the afternoon'. So at St Helen's, 'the two neighbouring Churches having duty in the afternoon', it was morning service that was said; and St Margaret, Walmgate, switched from afternoon to morning, 'as the three Churches on this side Foss-bridge . . . were all afternoon Churches and there was no Morning Duty in this part of the City'.

When there was a service, there was usually a sermon on at least one occasion during the course of a Sunday. The returns are not always clear on this point. Some clergy seem to have regarded a sermon as obvious so they forgot to mention it, even though they were asked; others may have wished to imply that they had only forgotten to mention in. Some were unclear as to whether they had one sermon which they preached twice or two sermons, offered in the same or different places. The duty of preaching was central to worship in eighteenth-century England and a good sermon was expected by congregations as well as the archbishop. At Leeds parish church, there were two sermons on a Sunday and sometimes one on a Friday as well, in addition to which on another weekday towards the end of the month a sermon endowed by Lady Elizabeth Hastings was given 'on the subject of the Sacrament of the Lord's Supper or on the duty of observing the holidays of the Church of England'. Sometimes, the congregation subscribed for a second sermon. At Fylingdales, a chapelry in the parish of Whitby, the incumbent was Richard Hauxwell, vicar of Sheriff Hutton. His curate was his son, William, who boarded in Robin Hood's Bay, performed divine service twice on a Sunday for his large chapelry of 320 families and delivered two sermons, the second paid for by subscription and doubtless a welcome addition to young William's income. Preaching could be a physically exhausting affair. Few preachers were as abstemious as Drummond himself at the Coronation in 1761 when he preached for about a quarter of an hour. Twice or three times this length would have been more usual. In the larger towns, a separate lecturer was sometimes employed to deliver an additional sermon. In Leeds, for example, Miles Atkinson, appointed curate to Samuel Kirshaw from 1766, was also lecturer at the parish church from 1770. Churches were designed essentially as preaching boxes and there was little to choose in this respect between the worship places of the Establishment and of Dissent. Though a later age of reformers was to frown on this view of the church building, by the standards and expectations of the day the Georgian church as a preaching church was doing its duty.

What is most striking about the information on services yielded by the visitation returns is not only the number of places which did have two services each Sunday with at least one sermon, but also how much else was also being organised by way of public worship. Though regular weekday services did not become common until the second half of the nineteenth century, nevertheless in 1764, fifty churches had services on Wednesdays and Fridays throughout the year and 188 of the 617 replies reported services on holy days. Lent was a special season, when 102 churches held Wednesday and Friday services. Two places - as different as the small parish of Thirkleby, three miles from Thirsk, and the large parish of Thornhill, five miles from Wakefield, held daily services during Lent and a further seven did so during Passion Week. In the larger towns, Doncaster, Pontefract, Wakefield and York, prayers were said daily throughout the year, while at St Mary's, Hull, and St John's, Leeds, there were two services each day and at Leeds parish church as many as three. High Church and Puritan traditions mingled with the new Evangelicalism to produce this varied pattern of worship. George Burnett, the curate at Elland in Halifax parish and a leading Evangelical, not only conducted two services every Sunday but also on Wednesday and Friday mornings, saints days and Wednesday evenings at seven o'clock. Henry Venn in Huddersfield held evening services at seven o'clock every Thursday. His curate, Samuel Furly of Slaithwaite, offered services every Wednesday at seven o'clock. In all, weekday services were held, seasonally if not throughout the year, in about a sixth of all the Yorkshire churches, including some in every major centre of population.

The service at which the Sacrament of the Lord's Supper was celebrated was an important but not frequent one in the eighteenth century. This is another aspect in which the later Victorian church displayed different values and expectations from those of the Georgian church and so assumed a false standard of judgement. High churchmen were usually satisfied with a pattern of monthly plus principal holy days - a frequency of celebration amounting to no more than sixteen times a year in all. Only a few clergymen, including John Wesley, were sufficiently sacramentalist to favour a weekly pattern, but this was the practice of Arthur Robinson at Holy Trinity, Hull. The Prayer Book norm was only three times a year, including Easter, to which Michaelmas was sometimes added to complete a quarterly pattern.⁹ Far from this infrequency suggesting a disregard for the sacrament, as in the Presbyterian tradition it suggested the opposite. Infrequency emphasised the unique importance of the occasion which was the climax to a week or longer of careful spiritual preparation. Samuel Kirshaw, vicar of Leeds, was one of several Yorkshire clergymen to follow the old puritan custom of holding a weekday service in preparation for reception of the Lord's Supper. Benjamin Wilson, the vicar of Wakefield, held both morning and afternoon services two days before communion Sunday. In 1743 there had been sixty places which held celebrations monthly; in 1764 the number was sixty-three. Much depended on the clergyman and local custom. Christopher Atkinson, for example, one of the original Oxford 'Methodists', celebrated only three times a year at Walton, but monthly in the next and more important parish of Thorpe Arch where he resided. All together, there were at least thirty-seven churches where the communion was administered eighteen times a year, and another eight cases where the information is ambiguous. When comparing the returns of 1764 with those of 1743, one finds at least seventy-four places where the Lord's Supper was administered more frequently at the later date and no more than twenty-seven where it was administered less frequently. This increased frequency was sometimes sponsored, as at Wentworth where Lady Malton (mother of the future second Lord Rockingham) paid the curate to institute monthly communion. Sometimes it may have been less than popular, as when Richard Conyers proposed a monthly Sacrament for Helmsley so that the alms collected could be applied to support a school for poor children. With 450 regular communicants Conyers was able to provide for 'near forty poor children', though some of his parishioners thought him an 'Over-doer'.¹⁰

Residence and Pluralism

One of the biggest problems that faced the Georgian church was the holding of livings in plurality. Of the 617 parishes and chapelries in the returns, only 273 (44 per cent) had resident incumbents, but the situation was not quite so bad as it seemed. For a start, in another seventy places there were resident curates. Secondly, only forty-four (7 per cent) livings were held as part of a threesome or more, so in most cases pluralism meant no more than two livings in the hands of one person. Thirdly, most of the visitation returns refer to plurally-held parishes only two or three miles from each other, well within the limit of ten miles that would be laid down in the Pluralities Act of 1838. The usual explanation for this was a combination of the smallness of population and the poverty of the living - the two often being connected. There were sixty-nine small parishes of less than fifty families with non-resident clergy and a value of under £20 a year, compared with twenty-five small parishes with non-resident clergy and an income of over £50 a year. Of the latter, only ten had incomes of over £100 a year.

There were many cases of near-residence. Of the sixty-nine small, poor parishes and chapelries, at least thirty-five, some of them with the same incumbent, were in the care of a clergyman who either lived close by or resided in another of his own parishes close by. Most of the other non-residents had curates in place, living either in or near the parish or chapelry. By contrast, of the small but wealthier parishes, only one incumbent lived in an adjacent parish. This difference suggests several patterns of pluralism, most of them not thought unacceptable at the time.

An extreme example of one clergyman who had accumulated poor livings in close proximity was James Addison, who ran a school assisted by his curate at Knayton in the parish of Leake, just over three miles from Thirsk. Knayton lay midway between the settlements of Cowesby and Over Stilton to the north-east, and Sandhutton and Carlton Miniott to the south-west. Addison was responsible, with his curate, for worship in all four communities, in addition to which he temporarily performed service also at Leake. Addison normally looked after the chapels at Sandhutton and Carlton, with the curate caring for Cowesby parish church and the chapel at Over Stilton. Somehow, by alternating services and expecting the Sandhutton and Carlton congregations to attend services in either chapel - they were only a mile apart - he managed to keep public worship going in all four villages, the total population of which amounted to only 123 families.

Boynton (21 families) near Bridlington, provides a similar example. Here John Knowsley was the resident incumbent curate; he also held

Carnaby (25 families), a mile and a half away; Fraisthorpe (12 families and worth under £10 a year), three miles away; Bessingby (20 families and worth under £10 a year), two miles away; and Burton Fleming (40 families and worth under £15 a year), five miles away. With a little help from the curate at Langtoft, for which he paid £9 a year, Burton Fleming got a service three times a month, Carnaby a morning service every Sunday, Boynton an afternoon service every Sunday and Fraisthorpe one every six weeks on a Sunday morning. The church at Bessingby, as explained earlier, had fallen down and there were no services there.

One incumbent who juggled four places of worship with less justification, since all four were parishes with a sufficient income, was John Bradley, who held in plurality Upper and Gate Helmsley, Warthill and Holtby, residing at the latter. Admittedly, the four churches were within a couple of miles of one another and the total number of families was only sixty-two, but the income was £135 a year. Bradley had no curate but expected his congregations to follow him around.

John Coates, who resided at Shipton, north of York, where he kept a school, was rather less open in his returns. He was responsible both for Newton-on-Ouse and for Nether Poppleton, about five miles away and on the other side of the river. He claimed to provide each village with a Sunday service on three Sundays in the month, and a double service at Newton the fourth Sunday in the month. What he did not admit to in any of his returns was that he was in addition the vicar of Acomb on the outskirts of York, where he also provided a weekly service. Although all three churches were with a few miles of one another and the total number of families was only 201, it is hard to see how Coates could have performed an effective ministry in all three places at once without the aid of a curate. It is perhaps not surprising that Acomb was an early centre of Methodist activity in York.[11]

With less excuse on grounds of income, Sidney Swinney held in plurality two of the wealthiest small livings, Barton-le-Street £100 and 40 families) to the west of Malton and Thwing (£180 and 34 families) to the west of Bridlington. These parishes were too far apart to be treated as one, but Swinney solved the problem by paying curates about a quarter of the incomes to look after each of the parishes while he lived in Scarborough. One curate took two services at Barton, which was one service better than in 1743, while the other curate held one service at Thwing, so the people of the two villages did not necessarily feel the consequences of pluralism and absenteeism. Scarborough also attracted George Dodsworth, whose two churches in the united vicarage of Allerston and Ebberston were looked after by the incumbent clergymen at Levisham who first did early morning service there before hurrying eleven miles to take a second morning service in either Allerston or Ebberston followed by an afternoon service in the other. Meanwhile, Dodsworth looked after the eighty-eight families at Cloughton and 124 in Scalby and Burniston for the vicar of Scalby. The latter was master of the grammar school at Beverley and lecturer at St Mary's, Beverley.

The most blatant yet most untypical instance of 'classic' pluralism was revealed in the return from Etton (£160) where the rector was Dr Hugh Thomas, also rector of Wheldrake (£140), archdeacon of Nottinghamshire (£61), Dean of Ely and Master of Christ's College, Cambridge. His Etton return was filled in by his curate who did not answer question five about whether and why the incumbent was non-resident, but the Wheldrake return shows that Thomas lived either in Ely or Cambridge. His curates in Etton and Wheldrake were each paid about a quarter of the income from the livings.

York, as usual, was a special case, since most of the city livings were poor as well as small. The twenty-two parishes were served by seventeen clergy, twelve of whom were either wholly resident in their parishes or lived elsewhere in the city. Of the remaining five, one was resident when not at his other parish at Hotham in the East Riding, one was resident when not at his rectory at Keyworth in Nottinghamshire, one was resident when not at his vicarage at Kirkby-cum-Broughton, near Stokesley in the North Riding, one was schoolmaster at Wheldrake, seven miles south-east of York, and one was resident at Great Ouseburn, thirteen miles north-west of York. Three of the five absentees had curates and another usually had one. Besides offering their parochial Sunday services, several of the York clergy also offered weekly prayers, two offered daily prayers and four did duty in the Cathedral.

Throughout the diocese as a whole very few churches and chapels were actually left without a clergyman of some sort, either resident or living near enough to ensure that in the vast majority of cases at least one service was said each Sunday. Though this was not to be good enough for the Victorian reformers, who insisted on a resident clergyman and two Sunday services each week to build up parochial loyalties, it nevertheless represented a reasonable achievement in an age when under-endowment rather than greed compelled many clergymen to accumulate a stipend as best they could.[12]

Catechising

The instruction of the young in the faith in preparation for Confirmation was one of the most important duties of a clergyman and the articles of enquiry were intended to ensure good practice in this respect, asking not only when it was done, but whether any exposition was used to aid understanding. Knowledge that Archbishop Drummond was likely to perform regular confirmation tours may have encouraged his clergy, but in any case few were likely to admit that they did not undertake this basic function of the church. Accordingly, of the 617 returns, only thirty-four responses did not mention catechism and there were good reasons for most of these, some of which have already been implied. For example, John Knowsley had no church in which to catechise at Bessingby and so he instructed these children and those at the Fraisthorpe chapel at Carnaby church. John Nessfield catechised his Birdforth children at Thormanby where he was resident, and this appears to have been the case also in several other chapels, the catechising taking place in the parish church.

Some of the omissions are surprising, given that they concerned clergymen known otherwise to have been diligent in the performance of their duties. The largest parish to have no regular catechising was Almondbury (1,800 families), next to Huddersfield, where the High Church incumbent, Edward Rishton, now old and blind, admitted that his age and infirmities had restricted him from regular catechising, though he had prepared 200 children for the confirmation visit made by Drummond to the area in May 1763.[13] Another offender was Henry Crooke, the Evangelical curate of Hunslet Chapel in the parish of Leeds (750 families). His explanation hints at the problem sometimes encountered in getting children to attend:

> When I first came to Hunslet I catechised every Sunday and continued to do so until I had only 2 children sent to me. I then removed the catechism from Sunday afternoon to Saturday nights in hopes of better success, which at first was beyond any expectation, the chapel being filled with hearers and no want of children to be catechised. This lasted only for a time and no children were sent, which discouraged me so much I have not catechised since. But 20 girls being lately sent from the foundling hospital into the skirts of my chapelry I purpose, God willing, to renew my catechising. My people are too backward in sending their children and servants to be instructed and catechised. When I catechised I used no exposition but endeavoured to speak as God was pleased to enable me.

Consumer resistance seems not to have been unusual. James Barwick, curate of Eskdaleside (25 families) had few children of the proper age and parents were backward in sending them. At Ebberston, few servants or children of the proper age were sent, and the curate seems to have found himself with 'chiefly small children'. At Brayton, the vicar sadly reported

> The parish lyes so wide that servants and children cannot be prevailed upon to come to say their catechism. I have repeatedly pressed them to come, more especially in Lent, when prayers are said twice a week, to no purpose.

The form of the question may have led some conscientious respondents to answer no when they meant yes, for it asked about catechising in church. This was the case with Samuel Johnson of St Mary's, Beverley, who was as old and infirm as Rishton of Almondbury, so he catechised not in church but in the vestry and only in preparation for a confirmation. This latter perhaps matched parental expectations, for in Sheffield, where the clergy catechised from Easter until Whitsun, they noted poor attendance except prior to a confirmation.

The expectation of the Prayer Book, embodied in the article of enquiry, was for catechising to take place in church, following the second lesson in the evening service. The customary season for this was Lent. Though most clergy did catechise, their replies show more variation in practice here than in any other answer, not least because in many churches only Morning Prayer was read. Also, to interrupt the service with catechism was not always practicable and congregations were anxious to get home before dark. So a variety of later seasons was offered: between Easter and Whitsunday, during April and May, Trinity Sunday, throughout the summer, at Harvest time. Whereas there was catechising throughout the year in over eighty churches, in as many it took place only during summer. Some incumbents catechised on weekdays in their parish schools. At Slaithwaite, Samuel Furly catechised between April and June on Saturday afternoons. In Leeds the process of catechising the entire township proceeded like a military operation, beginning on the first Sunday in Lent and continuing 'until we have gone through the town'. In Bradfield, a chapelry of Ecclesfield next to Sheffield, (534 families with two dependent chapels) the curate, finding his parishioners 'but too slack in sending their children and servants' took his message out to them, calling on 'particular neighbourhoods each Sunday till the whole be gone through'.

The teaching methods used were many and various. Some clergy were clearly puzzled by the idea that they might use an exposition and some replied with a vagueness that suggests their diligence in catechising might have been 'improved' for the archbishop's benefit. The phrase 'I know of no exposition which they make use of', found in the response from Skelton, represents a quite common approach which suggests catechumens being sent home to read up on the catechism, or perhaps an expectation that they might get help at home but that the provision of such assistance was no business of the clergyman. Other clergy gave out expositions for the children to take home but, as the rector of Addingham realistically commented, 'they may read them. I cannot tell.' Yet others - 197 in all - understood the question to relate to what aids they themselves used in their catechising, and were quite precise in their answers. W. Wake, *The principles of the Christian religion explained* (1699), W. Beveridge, *The Church Catechism explained* (1704) and J. Lewis, *The Church Catechism explained* (1732) were the most common. Other clergymen, with perhaps greater insight, adapted their approach to the children's minds. Joseph Hudson of Horton in Ribblesdale explained that 'formerly they learnt to repeat Lewis's catechism, but finding that too much of a task for the greatest part, I have read Dr Clark's exposition to 'em and occasionally several of the small Tracts given about by the SPCK.'[14] Thomas Newton of Carlton Husthwaite used a 'plain and familiar manner suitable to their capacities' and Abraham Clarke of Hawnby explained 'in as easy and familiar a manner as I possibly can'. Jonas Eastwood of Cleckheaton endeavoured 'to instruct them by a short explanation in the best manner I can'. Henry Venn of Huddersfield wrote his own exposition and then got the catechumens each week to repeat what they had learnt the week before. James Cookson of Aughton showed discrimination in encouraging preparation by recommending the children to read Lewis and their parents to read Wake. John Hinde of Fridaythorpe similarly 'recommended Lewis's and Dr. Stebbings' exposition for the better understanding of the church catechism to all masters of families'.[15]

The overwhelming evidence of the visitation returns is of widespread catechising activity across the diocese, in parishes small and large, urban and rural, by clergy who were young and old, High Church, Evangelical and neither. It is evidence of a genuine and continuing effort by the local representatives of the Established Church to bind their parishioners of the next generation into the fabric of the faith and worship of the nation. If they did not always succeed, it was not for want of trying.

Schools

Education was an act of charity and a religious duty. It was the responsibility of the Church to train up the children of England in wholesome doctrine with a proper sense of the Bible and of their station in life. School masters were to be licensed and thereby controlled by the bishop. By the mid-eighteenth century, though, theory and reality were coming apart. Obscure schools, often run by women teaching the basic elements of reading and perhaps writing or sewing, fell beneath the notice of the ecclesiastical authorities. Generally they were left alone if they did not appear a threat to the position of the church. Of more concern were those schools which had some formal, public existence, through endowment or regular public or private charitable support. Not only was the church interested in who taught what in such schools, but the parochial clergyman was also the best person to see that the money bequeathed or otherwise given for educational purposes in the parish was being properly used and accounted for.

The eighteenth-century grammar school was formerly, like the eighteenth-century Church, believed by historians to have failed, but by nineteenth-century standards rather than our own.[16] Grammar school endowments were intended to enable poor boys of the parish to become sufficiently learned in the classical languages to gain entry to the ancient universities. With the exception of the poor boy who aspired with the help of a local patron to tread this path to a career as a poor curate in the church, this original purpose was largely redundant. Boys from poor families needed basic education; those from more comfortable backgrounds could better use a modern, commercial education. Grammar schools had to compromise. The law, if observed, forbade the application of endowments to teaching modern subjects free of charge; but not to teach modern subjects might mean no pupils at all and certainly meant irrelevance to the needs of most families in the parish. In this way, some schools atrophied, others were transformed into petty schools for the poor, classical schools for the better off but not the poor, or modern schools. Some schools in more populous towns or with large and well-invested endowments, managed to survive by fulfilling several functions at once. This variety of types emerges in the visitation returns, and there is no consistency in what a school was called.

The church had a further interest in the school or schools of a parish. Often the only educated person qualified to run a classical school was a clergyman, and some school charters required this. Schools could thereby provide a useful sideline for a parish incumbent, or more usually his curate, especially if the living were poor or the allowance to the curate small. The parish school in this way often became an integral part of the work of the parish clergy. So the archbishop was keen to know as much as possible about 'any publick or charity-school, endowed or otherwise maintained' in the parish. He wanted to know when it was founded and by whom, who the master or mistress was, how many boys and girls were taught, and in what language (that is, English or Latin). He also wanted to know whether they were maintained and lodged; what they were taught, and what they went on to do afterwards 'in husbandry, trade or services'. But 'more particularly' he wanted to know whether there was 'care taken to instruct the children in the principles of the Christian religion, according to the Church of England, and to bring them duly to church as the Canon requires'.

The replies were as diverse as the parishes from which they came. Some respondents, like Cornelius Rickaby of Flamborough, bluntly wrote 'None'. Others, like John Hinde of Fridaythorpe, expanded a little: 'We have neither publick nor charity school taught' but went on to assure the archbishop in anticipation of a later question that 'The children are regularly catechised'. Many places lacked endowments. At Cotton, 'There is no public endowed school. A schoolmaster is occasionally hired and maintained.' Other places had inadequate and obscure endowments. At Dishforth Chapel, the vicar of Topcliffe recalled, there was an endowment - 'About 3 acres of land lying in the township of Topcliffe rented at £2. 15 shillings *per annum* left by whom, or when, cannot be discovered, for the encouragement of a school master at Dishforth and the present master's name is John Shaw. 6 poor children should be taught free in English or knitting or sewing but the salary being so small they are often without a schoolmaster.' By contrast, St John's, Beverley, had an endowment of £500 from Sir Michael Newton and £3 a year by the will of Mrs Ann Routh. A master was employed and nine boys were clothed, maintained and lodged, and taught English. They 'constantly' attended church and were catechised as required by the canon.

Some well-established and richly-endowed grammar schools continued to fulfil their historic purpose. In Leeds, the grammar school was founded in 1650. By 1764 its endowment was yielding an income of £200 a year, sufficient to fund a master and usher to teach ninety boys Latin and Greek. Both men in 1764 were graduates and clergymen. Drax had a charity school endowed by Charles Reed in 1669. The master, who was also the curate at Drax, received £30 a year and six poor boys were clothed every Christmas and their parents received £3 towards their maintenance. The boys were taught to read, write and cast accounts and then be put to some trade (except husbandry). In Almondbury, on the other hand, the ancient grammar school, refounded by royal charter in 1608, had fallen on hard times. The master was Samuel Brook, who had first been appointed in 1727, a year before his graduation from Cambridge, though he was not licensed to teach until 1732. At first he was curate of Marsden in Almondbury parish, but from 1738 held the curacy at Flockton in Thornhill parish, travelling the five miles between his school and his cure on horseback. The school was 'competently' but not well endowed and Brook was doubtless pleased to have the £48 income from Flockton to add to his £24.15 shillings from the school. Even so, he rebuilt the school house at his own expense. But in the 1750s old age caught up with Brook, 'afflicted many years with a nervous disorder, that, in the latter end of his time, bowed him almost together. Some called it Gout'.[17] He now travelled, painfully, by coach but made no mention in his return of his problems. Rishton of Almondbury, who had little to do with the school despite its being close by his church, was more brutally honest, describing Brook as 'so disabled by the gout and other infirmities that no children have been taught in it [the school] for several years'. The school survived but never really prospered. A second grammar school in the parish, endowed with £16.5 shillings at Holme, seven miles away, was also in crisis, the 'very worthy' master having just died. By contrast, Rishton's own curate, John Murgatroyd, was schoolmaster at the parochial school in Slaithwaite in the neighbouring parish of Huddersfield. This school illustrates the close involvement of the church in education. It had been started in the early 1690s by Robert Meeke, the curate of Slaithwaite from 1685 and endowed in 1721. Murgatroyd was master from 1738 and became curate of Almondbury in 1755. He remained at the school until 1786, teaching English subjects and Latin when needed.[18]

The overall impression gained from the returns is that in many parishes, education was being promoted within the financial limits of meagre endowments, and if these endowments sometimes acted as a subsidy to the curate, he in turn was enabled to bring some small amount of learning to a few boys who might otherwise not have had the experience.

The administration of charities

Closely allied with the good conduct of education was concern for the efficient and honest administration of all parochial charities. Small sums of money were available in well over half the Yorkshire parishes, usually administered by trustees of whom the incumbent was likely to be one. Opportunities for good works – and for misuse and corruption – were ever present.

Just over half of all parishes and chapelries (334) had some form of endowment, 174 of them in parishes where the living was worth £40 or less. In the towns, the endowments were sometimes considerable, with almshouses and hospitals. Beverley, St John had by the will of Ann Routh a hospital for twelve widows. Each had a room, an apartment for their fuel, a purple gown and silver badge, and two shillings a week, all under the control of the mayor and corporation. Doncaster had a hospital for six persons dating back to 1557, with a current income of £72 a year administered by the mayor, vicar and other trustees. Guisborough (over 300 families) had a hospital for six poor men and six poor women under the direction of a feoffee and two wardens. But even some small places had similarly endowed institutions. Coxwold (158 families) had two hospitals endowed by Thomas, Earl Fauconberg; and Halsham (32 families) had a hospital for eight men, each of whom received £4 a year, who were cared for by two women each paid £2 a year. Local aristocratic patronage was always likely to be an advantage, as was the case for the five poor men and five poor women of Ledsham who enjoyed the beneficence of Lady Elizabeth Hastings of Ledstone Hall, or the six old bachelors or widowers and six widows blessed by Lord Burlington at Londesborough. Much indeed depended on the accident of a local benefactor. Drax (100 families) was fortunate in Charles Reed who, in addition to his school, provided an alms house for each of three men and three women, a coat and a gown every two years at Christmas and £4 a year to live on.

More usual, though, was the comment from Bramham that 'There is no alms house or hospital endowed, but some benefactions left to the poor of the town and the parish, which are usually distributed by the vicar, churchwardens and Overseers of the Poor'. Some benefactions had strings attached. At Bramham Richard Tate's generous £12 a week was to be given to six poor people at church every Sunday, which would have discouraged religious Dissent. At Whiston, the dole was for people who attended church twice on Sunday. The penny in bread at Helmsley was for 'poor protestant people'. At Nunnington cash payments were for the poor who attended prayers on New Year's Day. Payment of these small sums in kind was common, either bread or clothing.

Not all such benefactions went to the poor. Nettleton's charity of 1613 left lands worth about £30 a year for trustees in Almondbury to employ in succouring and relieving the poor, repairing decayed bridges and highways, assisting in 'the preferment of the poor maids of the township in marriage', helping 'poor scholars born in the town of parents not able to prefer them', and for an almshouse which was not apparently built. One beneficiary was Samuel Brook, son of the schoolmaster, who went from the grammar school to St John's College, Cambridge in 1751 with eight guineas a year for four years.[19]

Among the more exotic uses to which charitable giving was put came in Patrington, where the benefaction was for the repair of old bell-frames and to pay the ringers on their annual perambulation of the parish.

Many of the reported benefactions were for the church or to augment the stipend of the incumbent. Again, the purpose of the article of enquiry was to make sure that the money had not been lost or diverted from its intended purpose. At Burton Agnes, Richard Green, a previous vicar, had endowed a school in 1563 and left £200 for the purchase of land to yield an annual income, fifty shillings of which was for church repairs and forty shillings for the poor. Among the many benefactions in Ecclesfield was land to be managed by feoffees to provide an income, in order of priority, for the maintenance of divine service in the parish church, the repair and ornamentation of the church, the relief of the poor, the repair of the highways, and such other uses as they thought appropriate. At Cross Stone in Halifax parish, one charge on a benefaction of land was ten shillings a year for the minister. Sometimes the endowment was for a specific sermon: eight shillings at Tickhill for a sermon on 1 August; 10 shillings at Himsworth for a sermon on 19 December; fifty shillings to the incumbent at Sledmere for a sermon on Christmas Day; and forty shillings to the curate at Tong for a catechising sermon.

Occasionally abuses came to light. At Lastingham several small sums for the poor had not been paid for years. At Hunslet, Henry Crooke had not received so much as one annual fifty-shilling payment from a charitable bequest since he had become curate there in 1749. Samuel Brook had even been to Chancery in 1753 to get a £5 benefaction left by Israel Wormall who died in 1737, but by 1764 he had still received neither the annual payment nor the arrears. At Seamer, the curate had not received sums due to him for preaching charity sermons in support of the children at the charity school, the money having been diverted partly to a dissenting minister two parishes away and partly to the descendants of the founder of the bequest. Thomas Barker of Leven was also having difficulty extracting from the heir the twenty shillings left by his father for the poor. The vicar of Scrayingham reported that he had taken matters into his own hands, rescuing the dwindling income from a benefaction to apprentice poor children, and investing the money in three per cent consolidated annuities at his own expense. In most cases there was probably little the archbishop could do to remedy reported alleged abuses when committed against rather than by his clergy. When the churchwardens of Pocklington complained that the vicar did not allow the curate 'a competent salary in proportion to the value of his living', the archbishop did nothing. One wonders how he reacted to the tactful hint of a potential abuse submitted by the vicar of Brodsworth:

> There is a tradition that a certain estate in the parish is chargeable with the repair of one aisle called Pickbourne Chancel, but as to the right, *quaere*

One suspects that Drummond was quite capable of distinguishing tradition from right, especially when he was the landowner in question.

Pastoral oversight

The sacrament of Baptism was the sign of entry to the church and was almost universally administered in childhood, the vows of the godparents being confirmed in front of the diocesan by the duly catechised child when he or she reached the age of sixteen. Adult baptisms were exceptions that had to be specially authorised by the bishop. This process was more than a formality. It went to the heart of what it meant for England to be a Christian country with an Established church. The archbishop therefore asked about it in his articles of enquiry.

The responses to this question are the most uninteresting of all the returns of the clergy. Five out of every six reported no irregularity, most simply repeating the words of the question in the answer: 'I do not know of any of this parish that are not baptised, nor being baptised and of a competent age are not confirmed or have not received the sacrament of the Lord's Supper. I have baptised no adults since your Grace became archbishop.' Occasionally a clergyman hinted at the problem of getting children confirmed at the right age. William Barrett of Askham Bryan admitted one irregularity: ' She was very desirous of it, but wanted an opportunity. It was in the time of your Lordship's immediate predecessor. She received the sacrament of the Lord's Supper several years since.' Thomas Lake of Bishop Burton was very precise, pointing out that those who had been just too young for Confirmation at the time of the last tour in September 1763, were now of age and not confirmed. A few incumbents were more realistic than the majority in recognising that, especially in the larger parishes, it was unlikely that all who were baptised would have been confirmed. Edward Rishton of Almondbury was being cautiously honest when he feared 'there may be some (but I hope not many) who are of a competent age and are not yet confirmed'. James Scott of Bardsey, non-resident but with a resident curate, was another realist who 'presume[d]' there were some who were baptised and not confirmed. A few of the clergy reported instances of adult baptism, mainly concerning former Quakers and Baptists whose parents' sectarian beliefs had precluded them from baptising their children as infants, though there were some instances - as at Wakefield, Pontefract and Darfield - of black servants being baptised as adults. At Bradford, James Sykes had baptised Patience and Anne Copley, aged nineteen and eighteen respectively, in preparation for their confirmation in 1763. At Batley, Thomas Scott had baptised Thomas Richardson, a former Quaker aged 55, three days before his marriage in December 1763. At Barnoldswick, Wilfrid Burton admitted to having several former Anabaptists, still unbaptised, in his congregation. The presence of Dissent in the large industrialising parishes ought to have meant the system expected in the article of enquiry was breaking down. If so, few were prepared to admit it as frankly as Thomas Colby of Birstall (1,700 families): 'Several come to church who are not confirmed, whose parents are dissenters of various denominations'. Marmaduke Teasdale of Brayton had one Methodist who occasionally came to church, 'but by what I can learn never was baptised'.

The other question concerning the beliefs and behaviour of parishioners was about the performance of penances imposed by the archdeacons' courts. The vitality of the church courts by the mid-eighteenth century varied from diocese to diocese and certainly overall they were not as important in the lives of parishioners as they had been in previous centuries. Anyone could start a case in the court. Civil disputes between individuals were less common than criminal cases, initiated by the officers of the court in response to a presentment (complaint) by the churchwardens or incumbent of the parish. Presentments were made at the time of a visitation by the archdeacon, and in his question Archbishop Drummond was interested only in whether any penances imposed had been performed since he became archbishop, a period of under three years.[20]

A survey over a longer period shows that in the archdeaconry of the East Riding, of 239 presentments between 1759 and 1773, only forty-five (19 per cent) could be described as other than for moral offences, the principal one being non-payment of church assessment (fifteen cases). The rest ranged from adultery and incest (two cases each) to fornication, which accounted for 152 or 64 per cent of all cases.[21] Most of the cases where details are given in the visitation returns, not unsurprisingly therefore, relate to fornication and most of the penitents were women. The word 'fornication' strictly speaking meant sexual intercourse between the unmarried but it appears to have gathered a wider sense in some of the returns, so that the curate at Great Ayton felt it necessary to specify that two penances performed in his church had been for 'antenuptial fornication'. At Adwick-le-Street Catherine Lawrence, a widow, performed public penance for having a bastard child, probably but not necessarily the result of fornication in its narrowest sense.

The incidence of public penance varied a great deal from parish to parish and it is hard to believe that this reflected accurately the morality of parishioners when five penances were generated by thirty-two families in Barmston but none by 537 families in Kirkheaton. Much may have depended on the zeal with which the churchwardens or incumbent carried out their duties, but even this was not necessarily so. At Bilsdale, 'regular presentments have been made by the churchwardens at every visitation' and yet no public penances had been performed; whereas at Danby, the churchwardens made regular presentments and 'penances were always performed as enjoined by the court', though the curate did not say how many of these there had been. Nor did he admit that complaints had been made about his own boisterous carousing and even incapability some Sundays of stepping into the pulpit.[22] Not all presentments led to a penance being imposed. Sometimes people were found to be innocent, or their excuses were accepted, or they were fined. At Bilbrough, the curate did not know what the outcome of a court appearance had been, so obviously it had not led to the requirement of a public penance.

Occasionally there are instances of clergy using the question about penances to make a complaint to the archbishop about fellow clergy, even though this would normally be done at the archdeacon's visitation. One of the most serious came from the vicar of Cantley, three miles from

Doncaster, who complained of the 'scandalous conduct of the lecturer of Doncaster who frequently attempts to preach when too drunk to speak articulately, and indeed by no means fit to appear in a pulpit at all'. However, the vicar of Doncaster made no complaint in his return, mentioning only that the lecturer gave the sermon at the Sunday afternoon service each week.

The purpose of a penance was public shaming, the penitent having to appear before the whole congregation barefooted and dressed in a white sheet, making public confession of his or her sin and repenting of it. Sometimes a penitent could commute this punishment for a sum of money, perhaps then performing the penance in private. The archbishop wanted to know if this had occurred and if so what had happened to the money. Most clergy who reported penances claimed there had been no commutations, but the rector of Bolton Percy revealed a scandal which cannot have been unique to his parish. His curate had granted some private penances for money, 'which a set of farmers talked of in such a manner in my hearing that I am persuaded they do great mischief rather than good, and tend to corrupt instead of reforming the morals of such people, for when the shame may be bought off at so easy a rate, they trouble not themselves about the sin'. They had, indeed, been discussing penances as 'mercantile wares'. Edward Rishton at Almondbury had a similar problem with his curate, Edward Hasleham, in the chapelry of Honley. Although Hasleham admitted to 'several' public penances in his return, Rishton was concerned that when Thomas Kirshaw and Elizabeth Bradley had been presented by his churchwardens for fornication leading to the birth of a bastard child, the woman had performed her penance in the parish church but the man had gone off to Honley and secured a private penance from Hasleham. Rishton hoped the archbishop would investigate, 'for it will be impossible to keep these large parishes in tolerable order if such enormous offenders be permitted in contempt of their proper ministers, to do private penance in private chapels'. Though the archbishop did follow this up, he did nothing to satisfy Rishton's indignation.[23]

Rishton's attitude to his parochial responsibilities may have been a little old fashioned in that he still expected to regulate the morals of some 1,450 families in his part of his huge parish, but there is sufficient evidence from about a sixth of all returns to suggest that the use of public penances to regulate the behaviour - particularly the sexual behaviour - of the people was by no means a thing of the past in mid-eighteenth century Yorkshire. The expectation expressed in the articles of enquiry and reflected in many of the answers was that, from cradle to grave, the people of England, distributed into parishes, were the responsibility of their appointed clergy in the Church of England by Law Established.

Protestant Dissent

In the 1660s the English Parliament attempted to restore the Church of England in its full powers as the spiritual face of the English state. Legislation identified the privileges of a subject with adherence to the church. Immediately this proved unworkable, with the expulsion of around a third of the clergy in 1662 for refusal to conform. Nonconformity was a fact of life, recognised by Charles II's Declaration of Indulgence in 1672 (which was intended mainly to benefit Catholics) and the Toleration Act of 1689 (which was intended mainly to benefit Protestants). Thereafter, whatever the legal definitions of Nonconformity and the legal requirement of all not exempted under the Toleration Act to continue to attend their parish church or parochial chapel on a Sunday and to participate in its sacraments, the gap between theory and reality could only grow wider.

Nevertheless, until the late nineteenth century, articles of enquiry and the replies of the clergy continued to assume that the Church of England was the norm and Dissent was an abnormality that one day might be remedied. In many parishes in 1764, this was not an unreasonable hope, for numbers of Protestant Dissenters were small and dwindling in the first half of the eighteenth century. Archdeacon Francis Blackburne of Cleveland kept a wary eye open for Catholics but hoped for a doctrinal realignment among Protestants that would recreate a truly comprehensive Established Church.[24] Most clergy simply believed the parish church was the natural home of all parishioners and all should return to it as their true mother church.

The first thing the archbishop wished to know in his articles of enquiry was about numbers of Dissenters and their meeting houses. It was his duty to regulate what he could not eradicate and he needed to know the size of the problem. Some clergy were doubtless reluctant to admit that they had a problem but most seem to have had a creditable knowledge of their parishes, either directly or through their curates. Most knew how many families they had care over and which of these were Dissenters. Only in a few cases or in the largest parishes does vagueness enter the replies, suggesting either unfamiliarity with the parish or numbers beyond reasonable estimate.[25] Even so, the overwhelming impression is of a clergy with a sound knowledge of their parishes.

In only eight of the 617 responses did the clergy not attempt to estimate the number of families in their parish. It is significant for how parishioners were perceived at this time that counting was still by family rather than by head.[26] Nearly half the returns in both 1743 and 1764 reported some Dissenters, and a quarter reported no Dissenters on either occasion. For the rest, sixty-eight seem to have lost their Dissenters by 1764 while eighty-eight places had gained them. Though there was doubtless some inaccurate reporting - intentional or otherwise - many of the returns look plausible, especially where small numbers were involved. The reporting from Huddersfield of about 100 families of Dissenters in both 1743 and 1764, or of 50 on each occasion at Barnoldswick, is probably less accurate than the three reported at Owthorne or the ten at Stokesley. Many parishes showed modest and plausible changes, as one or two families moved in or out of a parish, but in some places the change was too dramatic to be believable. In the parish of Halifax, the number of Quaker families fell from sixty to nine in the central township but increased slightly in other parts of the parish. One clear case of a misleading comparison comes in Kirkburton, which returned thirty Quaker families in 1743 and twenty in 1764, whereas Holmfirth chapelry in which the Wooldale Quaker meeting house was situated sent in no return in 1743 but recorded ten Quaker families in 1764. Here the 1743 return appears to have referred to the whole parish, while that of 1764 addressed only that part served by the parish church. Both decline and misleading reporting may have occurred in Calverley parish, where Presbyterian numbers fell from 230 to eleven families. Here the vicar explicitly excluded information from his two chapels at Pudsey and Idle from his 1764 return. Both Idle and Pudsey, unlike Calverley itself, had been strong centres of Dissent since the 1660s. Though Dissent in Idle had been in decline since before 1743 and fell from 102 to thirty families between 1743 and 1764, in Pudsey, which was not included separately in the 1743 returns, about two fifths of the 574 families in the township in 1764 were Dissenters, mainly Presbyterians and Moravians which in part reflected the arrival of the Moravians at Fulneck in 1744.[27]

Errors and ambiguities aside, some general statements can be made about the distribution of Dissent. In all, of the 389 returns reporting Dissenters in 1764, 256 named fewer than ten dissenting families in the parish or chapelry. Though many of these were small places, thirty-nine (15 per cent) of them had more than 200 families, making the dissenting element in these significant centres of population less than one family in twenty. On the other hand, of the fifteen replies reporting more than a hundred dissenting families, in eight the dissenting proportion was over one family in four. The highest incidence of reported Dissent came from Sowerby chapel in Halifax parish, with 451 out of 593 families (76 per cent) said to be Dissenters, including 188 Independents, 140 Presbyterians, and 56 Anabaptists.[28] Next came Batley with 418 out of 819 (51 per cent) and Cottingham with a suspiciously neat estimate that 'one half' of the 300 families in the parish was Presbyterian. It is certainly true that all three places were unusually strong centres of historic Dissent. In Batley parish the Presbyterians had succeeded in recapturing the chapel of ease in Morley in the early eighteenth century, a fact bemoaned by the vicar of Batley in his return, while in Gildersome chapelry the Baptists were strong and there was also a Quaker meeting house. In both chapelries, Dissenters outnumbered the Church. The other returns showing more than a quarter of families belonging to Dissent were Thornton chapelry in Bradford parish, Pudsey, Cross Stone chapelry in Halifax (actually on the outskirts of Todmorden), Bingley and Bradford itself. These were all highly populated areas of rapid industrialisation.

In seventeen returns showing between fifty and ninety-nine dissenting families, those with most Dissent relative to their overall size were either in industrialising parts of the West Riding, like Holbeck chapelry in Leeds, Wibsey in Bradford or Sowerby Bridge and Luddenden chapelries in Halifax, or old centres of Dissent like Barnoldswick, a strong Baptist centre, or both like Idle or Cleckheaton. Slightly different was the old North Riding market town of Yarm (283 families) on the crossing of the river Tees, where there were twenty-six Catholic, twenty-three Methodist and eleven Quaker families.

When plotted on a map of Yorkshire at large, the strongholds of Presbyterianism seem to have been in the major towns of the West Riding, such as Sheffield and Doncaster to the south and a cluster in the textile districts of the West Riding, around Wakefield, Bradford, Leeds and Halifax in the Calder and lower Aire valleys. In the East Riding, there were more than ten families in and around Hull, Cottingham and Beverley. In the North Riding, Whitby with sixty-three Presbyterian families out of 1699 stands out, perhaps because the curate there conducted an actual survey of his parish. York was also a major centre, with thirty-two families in the city but no more than three in any one parish. The Independents were historically less strong in Yorkshire and were often closely linked to the Presbyterians, expressing their distinctiveness only in the mid-eighteenth century as Presbyterian congregations split on Arian/Trinitarian lines. There were only twelve places recorded as having more than ten families of Independents, the strongest being Sowerby (Halifax), Hull (Holy Trinity), Leeds, Batley and Halifax. The latter had been at the centre of Independent strength since the time of Oliver Heywood who was ejected from Coley chapel in Halifax parish in 1662. The Baptists similarly congregated in this part of the West Riding, with seventeen places containing ten or more families, all in the Bradford and Halifax areas, reaching into the upper Aire and Calder Valleys where, in the early eighteenth century, the Baptist cause had been spread across the Pennines from Rossendale.[29] In that both Independents and Baptists adopted the Independent polity some clergy did not attempt to distinguish between them or, indeed, the Presbyterians. The return from Hunslet lumped Presbyterians and Independents together, and that from Keighley did the same for Presbyterians and Anabaptists. Henry Venn in Huddersfield reported that the sole Dissenting chapel in his parish was Independent with a congregation of about fifty. In fact it was a Baptist chapel. He also mistook the leading layman there for the minister.

Members of the Society of Friends were scattered across Yorkshire in small numbers, but there were twenty places where more than ten families were reported meeting, more places than for either the Baptists or Independents whose larger numbers were more concentrated. It may also have been that, with their distinctive form of worship and overt opposition to the normalities of parish life, the Quakers were easier for an incumbent to notice and count. Though they were strong where there were meeting houses in some of the expanding textile parishes of the West Riding, such as Leeds, Bradford, Guiseley and Kirkburton, there were also pockets of Quakerism in and around the North York Moors, in Kirby Moorside, Helmsley, Yarm and Whitby. York was also a centre, with twenty-six families in the city, and there were ten families in Hull. Quakers were also concentrated in Craven, the upland north-west of the West Riding, in parishes such as Keighley, Kildwick, Skipton, Slaidburne and Giggleswick towards the direction of the earliest Quaker meetings beyond the diocese in Sedbergh and on Pendle Hill.

All these areas of relative strength for the main branches of Protestant Dissent correlate partly with population density and large parishes, but equally important were smaller traditional locations of early Dissent with congregations dating back to the seventeenth century. Rooted in the major towns and scattered in the countryside there was little the Established Church could do about them. There is certainly no correlation between the presence of Dissent and infirm, non-resident or otherwise non-functioning clergy. The most one can suggest is that when an incumbent like Henry Venn in Huddersfield preached, people were said to have deserted the Baptist chapel to hear him. And when he departed, not only did the congregation at the Baptist chapel recover, but Venn's own followers with his encouragement established a private chapel of ease to continue the Evangelical tradition. This chapel soon drifted into Independency and became part of that movement for revival which breathed new life into the forms and patterns of older seventeenth-century Protestant Nonconformity.[30] But even Evangelical preaching could not rescue the Church of England. Venn himself estimated he had a hundred Dissenters in his parish, and in other industrial parishes with Evangelical clergy, Henry Crooke at Hunslet and John Eastwood at Cleckheaton also had numerous Dissenters, while rural parishes with Evangelical clergy, like Richard Conyers at Helmsley or Christopher Atkinson at Thorp Arch, had few.

Roman Catholicism

Protestant Dissent was, for the most part, an irritation. Roman Catholicism in 1715 and 1745 had been associated with a political threat to the monarchy and the country which the authorities in Church and State could not easily forget or ignore. Catholics were still subject to the recusancy laws and archdeacons and archbishops alike kept a watchful eye on them. What was apparent from the visitation and recusant returns is that, unlike the Protestant Dissenters, the Catholics had been growing in number during the eighteenth century. Though when examining the recusant returns in 1767, Drummond convinced himself that the lists taken in 1706 and 1743 had underestimated numbers, 'so that the Increase is not so great as appears at first sight', nevertheless he believed those numbers had grown by something like a third during the past sixty years. The point can be illustrated in the history of the city of York. Herring's figures for 1743 showed seventy families which, on applying Drummond's conversion ratio, can be taken as 350 persons, though 420 might be nearer the mark. The numbers reported by the clergy at the 1764 visitation were seventy-five families and nineteen persons – between 394 and 469 persons in all. At the 1767 count, Drummond actually found 642. This not only makes the points about growth and possible previous under counting; it also suggests that the clergy may have understated the presence of Dissent of all kinds in their visitation returns. The rector of St Michael le Belfrey in York, where the Catholic Mission was situated, reported a congregation of 170 at the mass house but only seven papist families in 1764. Three years later, the recusant returns listed 121 individuals in the parish.[31]

There were twenty-four other places in Yorkshire where more than ten Catholic families were reported. Most of these parishes were small and Catholics made up all or nearly all the Dissenters reported there. One cluster of Catholic families was to be found in Holderness in the vicinity of Burton Constable, in the parishes of Sheckling-cum-Burstwick, Aldbrough and Swine. Another was to the north of the North York Moors with Crathorne and Yarm in the west and Egton, Lythe and Whitby on the coast. Another string of parishes with more than ten Catholic families was to be found up the centre of Yorkshire from Carlton, Holme on Spalding Moor and Everingham in the south, through Sherburn-in-Elmet, Aberford, and Barwick-in-Elmet to York and thence through Newton on Ouse, Hovingham and Gilling to South Kilvington and Thornton le Street, just outside Thirsk. Another group ran west from York through Spofforth, Bishop Thornton (Ripon), Hampsthwaite and Ilkley, and then through south Craven to Mitton near Stoneyhurst on the county border.

None of these clusters of families was situated in the most populous and industrialising parishes. Several lay close to the seats of Catholic gentry families such as Burton Constable, Carlton, Everingham, Hazelwood, Gilling Castle and Stoneyhurst where domestic chaplains had laid the foundations for later missions. At Thornton-le-Street the vicar reported 'that Mr Rothwell, a Popish Priest and several Papists meet together every Lord's Day at the Hall of Roger Mennell Esqr at Little Kilvington in my parish'. The Meynells were one of the oldest established Catholic families in Yorkshire. The distribution of Catholicism, like that of older forms of Protestant Dissent, owed less to the practices of the Church of England in 1764 than to its historic roots. In the parish of Bishop Thornton, next to Ripley Castle, the twelve Catholic families constituted a quarter of the population – even though the Inglebys of Ripley had converted to Protestantism in 1617 and the male line of Catholic Inglebys at nearby Raventofts Hall had come to an end in 1720. But the Protestant heir, Stephen Ingleby, had allowed the missioner to continue and had provided a site for a house and chapel, where the Bishop Thornton Catholics were still meeting in 1764.[32]

Methodism

By contrast, historical patterns had little to do with the spread of Methodism, which was so new that many clergy did not know how to describe it. The figures given for Methodism are therefore too unreliable to be of much use. For example, only six Methodist families were declared in the twenty-two parishes of York in 1764, and yet four years earlier the Methodists of York had been sufficiently numerous to warrant building a chapel capable of holding between four and five hundred people. So all that can be gleaned from the visitation returns is a sense of the early distribution of Methodism and of clergy attitudes towards it.

One problem in identifying Methodists was that, in the words of the vicar of Calverley, 'Methodists baptize with us and come mostly to church'. John Wesley had always regarded his followers as auxiliary to the church and working within it, providing additional sermons and prayer meetings, and he exhorted all Methodists also to attend their parish churches. This practice was noted by the vicar of Bradford who reported that, unlike the Presbyterians, Baptists and Quakers who met for worship during the church service, the Methodists 'meet before and after the service of the church and usually attend at the church'. Such 'Church Methodism' was not only common in the mid-eighteenth century but was to continue in some rural areas for a further hundred years. Because, in the words of the vicar of Gisburn, 'the Methodists do not call themselves dissenters', where they had their own meeting places they did not see the need to register themselves under the Toleration Act. Though one need not accept the insinuation of the vicar of Darton, who believed that the Methodists 'conceal themselves', this refusal to behave as Dissenters did reduce their visibility. One can sympathise with the curate at Fylingdales, where the Dissenters comprised one Catholic family and one Quaker woman, 'unless the Methodists are so, which they absolutely deny'. They had a meeting house 'which is, they say, licensed, but did not choose to shew their license'. Another problem was the Methodists' lack of a fixed teacher. The Toleration Act presumed settled congregations and pastors. The Methodists, with their itinerant ministers, lay men and women preachers, and 'round' or 'circuit' system, were very hard to pin down. Thus the rector of Guiseley named no Methodist families in his parish even though there were two Methodist meeting houses, 'one in Yeadon and one in Guiseley, but neither of them licensed, neither have they any stated preacher at either of them nor fixed time of assembling'. This is what the curate at Guisborough meant when he wrote that 'They are taught by vagrant Methodists'.

Some clergy had their own reasons for not wishing to say more about the Methodists. The vicar of Bilton reported as though it would spoil his record to acknowledge them: 'I have about 120 families in my parish, amongst whome there is only 1 dissenter, which is a papist. If those that call themselves Methodists are to be deemed such there are about 7 of them more'. To admit to Methodists might suggest criticism. This comes through in the response from Thomas Bright of Ecclesfield. After mentioning four popish and two Quaker families, his return refers to

> a few dissenters enthusiastic or Methodists, cannot ascertain the number. I believe there are not so many as I found upon my first coming hither, though they swarm at present in the next neighbouring parish to me towards the south, namely Sheffield.

The comment of the vicar of Sheffield illustrates the ambiguous identity of these Methodists: 'their congregation is a Great concourse of people consisting of some from every other Sect and many who profess to be members of the established Church of England'.

Some Evangelical clergy saw no need for a separate Methodist effort in their well-run and evangelised parishes and so acknowledged none. So there were no Methodists reported in Henry Venn's Huddersfield or its chapelries at Slaithwaite and Scammonden. Although Dr Legh in Halifax and his curates in some of the Halifax chapelries acknowledged approaching a hundred families of Methodists, George Burnett, the Evangelical curate in Elland, did not include any among his Dissenters but merely reported 'There are also some licensed houses for Methodists. Their numbers very small'. Similarly in Leeds parish, though there were approaching a hundred and fifty Methodist families in Leeds township and Holbeck, Henry Crooke at Hunslet chapelry reported only Presbyterians and Independents, Quakers and Catholics.

Interesting light is thrown on relationships between Methodists and Church of England clergy in the return from Edward Rishton at Almondbury. This large, sprawling Pennine parish reaching across three valleys and including three chapelries, adjoined the parish of Huddersfield along the river Colne. Unlike Venn, Rishton was an old High Churchman who had no time for Methodism; neither had his curates. Venn's curate in Slaithwaite in the Colne Valley was Samuel Furly, an Evangelical in the Arminian mould of Wesley rather than the Calvinism of his vicar. Slaithwaite was not only a township in the parish of Huddersfield but a village astride the river Colne, including parts in the townships of Linthwaite and Lingards in Almondbury parish. Furly's chapel stood on the river bank, a literal stone's throw from Lingards, and served the townships on both sides of the river. Next to the chapel stood the village school, the school master of which was Rishton's curate who was probably responsible both for the beautiful copperplate script on Rishton's return and the information it reported at second hand. Having declared ten families of Dissenters in Almondbury, Rishton went on

> The Methodists, I am told, are pretty numerous in the remoter parts of this parish, but they are such a vagrant sect that it is impossible to give any account of them and besides they will not allow themselves to be called dissenters.

– which would be why Furly declared none in his return for Slaithwaite. In response to the next question about meeting places and teachers, Rishton went on:

> There are no licenced or other meeting houses in this parish, if I am to except the Methodists. But of them there are teachers without number. I am told, and believe it to be true, that the curate of Slaethwaite holds what he calls lectures, but I call conventicles, in two different towns in this parish.

Rishton continued to be plagued both by Furly and the Methodists, but when he complained further to his archbishop, Drummond – although no lover of enthusiasm – mildly advised that he knew 'no better way to resist the artifices of the deceivers than by plain instruction in the genuine doctrines of Christianity, and constant attention to the parochial duty'.[33]

Despite the inability or reluctance of many clergy to identify or number their Methodists, 113 returns (18 per cent) contain some reference to them. Of these, twenty-eight are imprecise and may refer to small numbers, as in Staninton (Bradfield chapelry, six miles from Sheffield) where 'a few in that quarter are tainted with Methodism' but others clearly refer to a substantial Methodist presence as in Sheffield itself where they were the 'most numerous' sect among a 'very large' number of Dissenters. Of the rest, thirty-one returns reported ten or more Methodist families, with the largest counts being in Batley (123 out of 819 families) and Bradford (103 out of 1,811 families). Like James Wilkinson of Sheffield, Samuel Kirshaw of Leeds made no attempt to estimate their number, not least because many also came to church.

The striking thing about Methodism is the extent and range of its appeal. Even given the problems of definition, clergy identified almost as many communities with ten or more Methodist families as they did for the Presbyterians, and more than for any other branch of Dissent. Despite the undoubted under-reporting, Methodism must already have been on its way to becoming the largest body of Dissent from the Established Church in Yorkshire. Though early Methodism was notorious for its strict discipline, which meant that membership numbers were far smaller than numbers for those influenced by Methodism, in 1766 the York Circuit, which included all the East Riding and reached in the North Riding as far as Thirsk and Whitby, had nearly a thousand members.[34] Places with more than ten families included not only the expected cluster around Leeds, Bradford and Halifax, and older centres of Dissent like Yarm, but also parts of the county in which Dissent had not previously been widely reported. In Pateley Bridge (519 families), Dissent was represented by one Catholic family and 'a great many' Methodists. Tadcaster (340 families) had fifteen Methodist families, six Catholic and two Quaker. In Northallerton, (610 families) all but six of the twenty-six families of Dissenters were Methodist. In a number of places, apart from a few Catholics or Quakers, Methodism represented the only Dissent in the parish. In Stillington, north of York, twenty of the eighty-five families were described as 'Protestant Dissenters called Methodists', but otherwise there were only two Catholic families. The same preponderance of Methodists was true of Hutton Rudby (169 families), where Wesley preached to a 'huge congregation' on Easter Monday 1764. The clergyman, George Stainthorpe, was not alarmed by this and wrote in his return that there were a hundred Methodists 'joined in society', but declared as Dissenters only three Catholics, two Quakers and one Anabaptist. At Kirby Wharfe, south of Tadcaster, of ninety-two families one was Catholic and fifty were Methodist. Here the explanation lies in the scattered nature of this rural parish, which contained two villages. The parish church was in Kirby Wharfe itself and here the church was supreme. The Methodists met in Ulleskelf, a mile away where there was no church and a local farmer led the Wesleyans and a labourer led a group of followers of Benjamin Ingham.[35]

Like Catholicism and Quakerism, Methodism could be a rural form of religion; like Presbyterianism and Independency, it could appeal in the towns. Like the Baptists it could attract support in the upland Pennine valleys of rapid industrialisation. The evenness of this appeal is illustrated in the figures supplied by Thomas Scott of Batley. In Batley itself, the Independents were strong with fifty-one families but the Methodists had forty-nine. In Morley, the Presbyterians were the most numerous with 129 families (compared with seventy-two in the Established Church) but the Methodists had forty-seven. In Gildersome, where the Baptists were strong with sixty families, the Methodists had twenty-three. Only in tiny Churwell, with sixty-eight, families, forty of them in the Church and twenty-two Presbyterian, did the Methodists come a poor third with four. As a result of this evenness across almost all the chapelries, the Methodists were second only to the Presbyterians in the parish as a whole - and this was a parish in which for historic reasons the Presbyterians were unusually strong.

Methodism, therefore, presents a different profile to the other forms of Dissent and was a far greater threat to the Church of England once it began to emerge as a separate denomination. Because it had grown up largely within the Church and operated through a circuit system with itinerant ministers and local lay preachers, it mimicked the Church in its coverage of the county and diocese as a whole. It grew strong not where it had historic roots but where the Established Church left an opening for it - where a parochial clergyman was an absentee, where there was only one service on a Sunday and the people wanted two, where a village in a large parish had no church or chapel of ease, where the congregation wanted to sing instead of saying the appointed psalm, where the sermon was dry or formal and the people wanted enthusiasm.

Conclusion

The challenge of Methodism is there in the visitation returns for the historian to see, but it was sufficiently hidden for many contemporaries, including the archbishop, not to see it. They did not have the gift of foresight nor the benefit of hindsight. Later reformers had the latter if not the former and judged accordingly. By the standards of his day, Drummond was a good archbishop. He meets few of the criteria set out by Peter Virgin for the 'typical Georgian prelate'.[36] He had not been promoted late in life; he was not old and infirm when coming to York; though his see was not poor it was not the richest but he could afford to enjoy it and even spent his own money improving his palace; though his see was large, he had capable archdeacons to help; though he did his parliamentary duty as expected he also spent time in the diocese, not least because his own home was at Brodsworth; he seems to have relished his tours of the diocese, even volunteering for one before he became archbishop; he was a capable administrator.

He did not even entirely lack vision, though he perhaps lacked the pertinacity to deal with large problems as effectively as he dealt with small ones. In the major question of restructuring the church in the American colonies and providing it with an episcopal structure, he worked hard with Archbishop Secker of Canterbury, only to be thwarted by politicians who had the final say in such matters. If he had had the same vision to see how the large industrialising and increasingly populated parishes of the West Riding needed restructuring, he might also have seen that there were too many vested interests, in religion and politics, to allow anything to happen. Indeed, even the Victorian reformers, with the backing of parliament, found restructuring the parishes slow and hard work. If he had realised the plight of poor curates and the need to enhance the value of livings to secure a resident clergyman in every church and chapel of every parish, he would also have known from his careful administration of Queen Anne's Bounty that there would never be enough money for this without the sort of massive parliamentary grants and private donations from which the nineteenth century church was to benefit. If these might-have-beens did occur to him, he quickly grew disillusioned. The large leather-bound book which the archbishop possibly prepared for a review of the outcome of his visitation is virtually unwritten in. The few entries suggest he might have been pondering a rationalisation of the parochial structure in York. If so, then something like his ideas was not to be implemented until the 1880s.[37]

Though the eighteenth century was a time of great social and economic change, it was not one in which most well-established and comfortable people sought change for its own sake, and Robert Hay Drummond was not one to do so. Neither were most of his clergy. When he confronted one who was, in the street in Malton during the visitation, he is reported as having addressed him ironically, 'Well, Conyers, you have given us a fine sermon! . . . If you go on preaching such stuff you will drive all your parish mad. Were you to inculcate the morality of Socrates, it would do more good than canting about the new birth.'[38] Conservatism seemed the safest course for a church unaware that this was not an option.

Measured against the findings of Archbishop Herring's returns, twenty-one years earlier, the returns of 1764 do not bear out Ollard and Walker's assertion that the mid-eighteenth century Church was losing ground. It was gaining and losing, but overall it was maintaining its position. Most parishes and chapelries had a resident or near resident clergyman, even if he were only a poor curate; most churches had at least one service on a Sunday, even if many did not have two. The Lord's Supper was administered as frequently as expected, with the monthly pattern being not uncommon, especially in towns. Most clergy catechised their young people. Again in the towns, additional services and prayer meetings were held with greater regularity than has often been realised. The old High Church tradition was still alive. The new Evangelicalism was stirring the church. During the 1770s the number of applications for Dissenters' Meeting House licences expanded rapidly, and began to shift from applications to licence rooms to the registration of chapels.[39] If Archbishop Drummond had still been alive twenty-one years after his primary visitation he would have found a very different picture from that presented in 1764. The returns of 1764 give us a last opportunity to glimpse a church which was still coping with the demands of the world and still confidently doing its spiritual duty.

Notes to Text

References to Archbishop Drummond's visitation returns (BIHR, Bp V 1764/Ret) are not given for individual parishes and chapelries. The returns for places referred to can be located in alphabetical order in ten bound manuscript volumes at the Borthwick Institute (with three further volumes for parishes in the archdeaconry of Nottingham). Transcriptions of the Yorkshire returns are currently being published in three volumes in the Borthwick Texts and Calendars series, edited by Cressida Annesley and Philippa Hoskin (1997 -).

1. S. L. Ollard and P. C. Walker, eds, *Archbishop Herring's visitation returns, 1743*, 5 vols (Yorkshire Archaeological Society, 1929-31)
2. N. Sykes, *Church and State in England in the XVIIIth Century* (Cambridge University Press, 1935). Among the most recent contributions to the debate are P. Virgin, *The Church in an Age of Negligence. Ecclesiastical Structure and Problems of Church Reform, 1700-1840* (James Clarke, 1989), J. Walsh, C. Haydon and S. Taylor, eds, *The Church of England, c.1689-c.1833. From Toleration to Tractarianism* (Cambridge University Press, 1993), and M. Smith, *Religion in Industrial Society. Oldham and Saddleworth, 1740-1865* (Oxford University Press, 1994).
3. In Judith Jago's original database, returns from 621 clergy were recorded, but eight of these represented four pairs of clergy from parishes held in moiety - Burnsall, Darfield, High Hoyland and Linton. These have each been counted only once in the statistics used in this paper.
4. J. Cannon, *Aristocratic Century. The Peerage in Eighteenth-century England* (Cambridge University Press, 1984), pp. 61-3.
5. J. Jago, *Aspects of the Georgian Church. Visitation Studies of the Diocese of York, 1761-1776* (Associated University Presses, 1997), p. 58.
6. Ibid., p. 42.
7. Ibid., pp. 69-70.
8. BIHR, Bp C & P VII/326, Mulso to Drummond, 11 May 1764.
9. For a summary of eighteenth-century attitudes to the Communion, see Henry Rack, *Reasonable Enthusiast. John Wesley and the Rise of Methodism* (Epworth Press, 1989), pp. 19-21.
10. BIHR, VR 1764, Helmsley, Conyers to Drummond, 17 May 1764.
11. J. Lyth, *Glimpses of Early Methodism in York* (William Sessions, 1885), pp. 55-6.
12. For Victorian expectations, see the comments of the Rural Dean for the City and Ainsty of York, ms. report, BIHR, R.D.AIN.1, pp. 167-8.
13. Rishton had virtually retired on the job, preaching his farewell sermon on 20 April 1762, though not dying until 29 December 1766: see the Rev. John Murgatroyd's Commonplace Book, vol. 2, quoted in C. A. Hulbert, *Annals of the Church and Parish of Almondbury, Huddersfield* (Longman, 1882), p. 478.
14. S. Clarke, *An Exposition of the Church Catechism* (1729).
15. H. Stebbings, *The Young Christian Instructed*, 9th edition (1756).
16. R. S. Tompson, *Classics or Charity? The dilemma of the eighteenth-century grammar school* (Manchester University Press, 1971).
17. Rev. John Murgatroyd's Commonplace Book, vol. 2, entry for 6 February 1771, quoted in C. A. Hulbert, *loc. cit.*, p. 480.
18. C. A. Hulbert, *Memorials of Slaithwaite Free School*, reprinted in *Three Huddersfield Diaries* (Toll House Reprints, 1990).
19. G. Hinchliffe, *A History of King James's Grammar School in Almondbury* (The Advertiser Press, 1963), pp. 46, 80. The lack of an almshouse in 1764 may be one reason why Rishton said the list of charitable intentions was 'too long to be here mentioned' and asked the archbishop to rely upon the trustees as 'all men of honour'.

20 For the operations of the church courts, see W. M. Jacob, *Lay People and Religion in the Early Eighteenth Century* (Cambridge University Press, 1996), pp. 137-54.
21 Jago, *op. cit.*, pp. 214-15.
22 *Ibid.*, p. 110.
23 BIHR, Bp C & P VII/376, Rishton to Drummond, 17 November 1764.
24 M. Fitzpatrick, 'Latitudinarianism at the parting of the ways: a suggestion' in Walsh, Haydon and Taylor, eds, *The Church of England*, pp. 209-27.
25 For example, the vicar of Sheffield excused himself with the words, 'The Populousness of this Town and Parish and the manner of living among the common People, several Families frequently Inhabiting the same House, have made it impracticable for me to ascertain precisely the Number of Families'.
26 When dealing with his recusant returns in 1767 Drummond used a multiplier of five to convert numbers of families into overall population figures: BIHR, Bp. Rec. Ret., 1767/B/2, Number of Papists or reputed Papists in the Diocese of York.
27 J. G. Miall, *Congregationalism in Yorkshire* (John Snow, 1868), pp. 294-6 (Idle) and 334-7 (Pudsey).
28 The return here is ambiguous. It is possible that it refers to numbers of individuals and not families, in which case only 15 per cent of the 3040 individuals in the parish were Dissenters. On the other hand, of 1533 individuals over the age of 16 only 70 made their Easter Communion at the parish church so a very low percentage of adherents to the Established Church is plausible.
29 W. E. Blomfield, 'Yorkshire Baptist Churches in the 17th and 18th Centuries' in *The Baptists of Yorkshire* (William Byles, Bradford, 1912), pp. 73-97.
30 J. Stock, *History of the Baptised, Independent and Congregational Church, meeting at Salendine Nook chapel, Huddersfield* [1874], pp. 10-18; R. Bruce, 'Congregationalism in Huddersfield', *Congregational Yearbook*, 1875, pp. 120-4. See also H. Venn, ed., *The Life and a Selection from the Letters of the late Rev. Henry Venn . . .* (John Hatchard, 1836), pp. 44-5.
31 BIHR, Bp. Rec. Ret. 1743/1, Number of Popish Families returned by the Incumbents in 1743. City of York and Ainsty; Bp. Rec. Ret. 1767/B/1-2, Number of Papists in the Diocese of York, and Number of Papists or reputed Papists in the Diocese of York; Bp. Rec. Ret. 1767/B/9, Parishes with the greater number of Papists.
32 H. Aveling, 'The Catholic Recusants of the West Riding of Yorkshire, 1558-1790'. *Proceedings of the Leeds Philosophical and Literary Society, Literary and Historical Section*, X part vi (September 1963), pp. 256-67, esp. 261. See also J. Bossy, *The English Catholic Community, 1570-1850* (Darton, Longman and Todd, 1975), pp. 82-91.
33 Drummond to Rishton, 24 November 1764. The text of this letter is given in C. A. Hulbert, *Annals of the Church in Slaithwaite* (Longman, 1864), p. 74, though Hulbert misread the date as 1769. Rishton had sent the letter in disgust to Murgatroyd whose papers were available to Hulbert. For the letter which occasioned this reply, and Drummond's note of the reply, see BIHR, Bp C & P VII/376, Rishton to Drummond, 17 November 1764.
34 J. Lyth, *op. cit.*, table on p. 154.
35 Ingham, one of the Oxford Methodists, was married to Lady Margaret Hastings of Ledstone Hall and lived nearby at Aberford Hall: see H. M. Pickles, *Benjamin Ingham* (privately printed, 1995).
36 Virgin, *op. cit.*, p. 159.
37 Jago, *op. cit.*, pp. 82-4.
38 Quoted from [A. C. H. Seymour], *The Life and Times of Selina, Countess of Huntingdon*, 2 vols (1840), II p. 280. Richard Conyers had just preached the visitation sermon.
39 See the entries in the Faculty Books for this period, BIHR, Fac.Bk. I-III.